Guglielmo Marconi

John Malam

Chicago, Illinois

HEINEMANN-RAINTREE

TO ORDER:
☎ Phone Customer Service **888-454-2279**
💻 Visit **www.heinemannraintree.com** to browse our catalog and order online.

Customer Service 888-454-2279
Visit our website at www.heinemannraintree.com

Edited by Louise Galpine and Catherine Clarke
Designed by Kimberly R. Miracle and Betsy Wernert
Picture research by Mica Brancic and Helen Reilly
Originated by Modern Age
Printed in China by Leo Paper Group

ISBN-13: 978-1-4109-3230-3 (hc)
ISBN-10: 1-4109-3230-3 (hc)

13 12 11 10 09
10 9 8 7 6 5 4 3 2 1

Library of Congress Cataloging-in-Publication Data
Malam, John, 1957-
  Guglielmo Marconi / John Malam.
    p. cm. -- (Great scientists)
  Includes bibliographical references and index.
  ISBN 978-1-4109-3230-3 (hc)
  1. Marconi, Guglielmo, marchese, 1874-1937--Juvenile literature. 2. Inventors--Italy--Biography--Juvenile literature. 3. Radio--History--Juvenile literature. I. Title.
  TK5739.M3M26 2008
  621.384092--dc22
    [B]
                        2007050126

Acknowledgments
We would like to thank the following for permission to reproduce photographs: © Alamy **p. 15** (Ilene MacDonald); © British Library Newspapers **p. 24** (The British Library); © Camera Press **p. 29 left** (S/T/B/SLondon); © Corbis **pp. 7** (Hulton-Deutsch Collection), **14** (Hulton-Deutsch Collection), **23** (Hulton-Deutsch Collection), **30** (Leonard de Selva), **39** (Bettman), **41** (Kevin Dodge); © From the Collections of RMS-Republic.com **p. 26**; © g4ftc.com **pp. 9, 12, 13**; © Getty Images **pp. 11** (Hulton Archive/Keystone), **27** (Hulton Archive/Edward Gooch), **34** (Hulton Archive/Topical Press Agency), **35** (Time Life Pictures), **36** (Time Life Pictures/Pix Inc.), **37** (Time Life Pictures/Pix Inc.); © istockphoto **p. 5** (Marcy Smith); © Mary Evans Picture Library **p. 4** (Illustrated London News); © Science & Society **p. 17** (Royal Photographic Society); © Science Photo Library **pp. 6** (Sheila Terry), **8** (Sheila Terry), **10, 18, 31** (Library of Congress), **33** (Library of Congress); © The Bridgeman Art Library **p. 19** (Archives Larousse, Paris, France, Giraudon/French Photographer); © The Fr Browne Collection **p. 29** right (The Irish Picture Library); © The Frith Collection **p. 22**; © The Kobal Collection **p. 28** (20th Century Fox/Paramount/Merie W. Wallace); © The Marconi Archives/The Bodleian Library **pp. 21, 25**.

Cover photograph of Guglielmo Marconi c. 1900 reproduced with permission of © Corbis.

We would like to thank Nancy Harris for her invaluable help in the preparation of this book.

CONTENTS

Some words are shown in bold, **like this**. You can find out what they mean by looking in the glossary.

WORLD WITHOUT WIRES

In the 1890s, a little known scientist, Guglielmo Marconi from Italy, discovered a new way of sending messages. Until Marconi's incredible discovery, there were three main ways to send messages:

- By letter. A letter could take days, weeks, or even months to reach the end of its journey. Some letters never arrived, because they were lost in fires or shipwrecks.

- By **telegraph**. This was faster than sending letters. Telegraph messages were sent in code along overhead wires and undersea cables. When they reached their destination, they were changed back into words, written out, and then delivered, just like letters.

This photograph of Guglielmo Marconi sitting in his study was taken in 1912, when he was 38.

- By telephone. This was also fast and, better still, it did not use code. Instead, people talked to each other—the sound of their voices traveled along telephone wires. But the telephone was a new invention, and few people had one.

Invisible waves

Marconi's discovery also sent messages quickly, and it could send them across continents and over oceans. He had found a way of sending messages through the air using invisible **radio waves**, instead of along hard wires or cables. This was Marconi's breakthrough. The scientist no one had heard of had discovered how to send **wireless**, or radio, messages. Marconi had found a new means of communication, and he became famous worldwide.

Cell phones are a common sight in today's wireless world. Marconi helped to make them possible.

Today's wireless world

It is thanks to Guglielmo Marconi that today's wireless devices are possible. Cell phones, portable radios, and computers all use wireless technology.

The family home
The Villa Griffone was a big house with lots of rooms. It was in the country, surrounded by orchards and vineyards.

Villa Griffone is where Guglielmo spent his early years. He carried out his first experiments here.

Early years
Guglielmo Marconi was born on April 25, 1874, in the city of Bologna, in northern Italy. He came from a well-known family who owned a lot of land. The Marconis were quite wealthy. They owned a large country house near the village of Pontevecchio, a few miles from Bologna. The house was called Villa Griffone.

Guglielmo's family
Guglielmo's parents were Giuseppe and Annie. Guglielmo had a brother, Alfonso, and a half-brother, Luigi. Alfonso was 9 and Luigi was 19 when Guglielmo was born. His father, Giuseppe, was Italian. His mother, Annie, Giuseppe's second wife, was from Ireland. She came from a rich family. Her family had been successful in business.

Guglielmo, Alfonso, and their mother traveled a great deal when Guglielmo was young. They spent winters in Florence or Livorno, in central Italy, returning to the Villa Griffone every summer.

Guglielmo learned to read and write in Italian and English. His mother read to him in English, and when his English-speaking cousins came to stay at the Villa Griffone, he spoke English with them. He had a talent for music, and his mother taught him to play the piano, which he was good at.

Homeschooling

He was sometimes educated by tutors at home, but he found the classes boring. This attitude worried his father, who expected him to do well with his schoolwork. Giuseppe wanted his son to become an officer in the Italian navy—and that required performing well in school.

Guglielmo, at about four years old, is on the left of this photo. His mother and brother Alfonso are also shown.

A passion for science

There was one subject that did hold Guglielmo's interest—science. He particularly liked reading books and magazine articles about electricity.

In the 1880s electricity was quite a new subject, and scientists were still discovering ways to use it. For Guglielmo, electricity represented the most up-to-date technology in the world, and it must have seemed incredibly exciting to him. His family did not understand why he was so interested in electricity. They may have thought that he would soon grow out of his unusual interest. He did not.

Guglielmo's experiments

Guglielmo soon began to carry out experiments with electricity. He read about Benjamin Franklin, a U.S. scientist who had proved that lightning is a form of electricity. This inspired 13-year-old Guglielmo to make his own lightning **conductor**— a device to attract lightning. He set it up at the side of the road, with a wire running from it to a bell in the house. Each time lightning struck the conductor, it created a charge of electricity that traveled along the wire and rang a bell inside the house.

This painting shows what Benjamin Franklin might have looked like flying his kite in a storm as part of an experiment.

In addition to being educated at home, Guglielmo took private classes at a school in Livorno. A professor there, Vincenzo Rosa, taught him about **physics** and, in particular, **electrophysics**.

Electricity firsts

1831 First electric telegraph machine, invented by Joseph Henry, in the United States

1866 First successful Atlantic telegraph cable laid, connecting Great Britain and the United States

1876 First electric telephone, invented by Alexander Graham Bell, in the United States

1878 First electric light bulb, jointly invented by Joseph Swan, in the United Kingdom, and Thomas Edison, in the United States

1881 First electric streetlights, in Godalming, United Kingdom

1883 First public electric railroad, in Brighton, United Kingdom

This modern replica of Marconi's lightning conductor is on display at the Villa Griffone.

Messages along wires

When Guglielmo was about 16, he met an elderly blind man. Guglielmo became Nello Marchetti's eyes, reading books and newspapers to him. In return, Marchetti, who had worked as a **telegraphist**, taught Guglielmo Morse code. This was a communication system in which each letter of the alphabet became a pattern, or code, made from dots and dashes. Telegraphists learned the code by heart. As they tapped it out letter by letter, coded messages were sent in the form of electrical energy along telegraph wires.

Global communication network

By the 1890s, when Guglielmo learned Morse code, the telegraph **network** spanned the globe. Wires and cables stretched their way around the world. They connected towns and cities to a global communication network— the first in history.

This is a portrait of Samuel Morse. His communication system changed the way messages were sent around the world.

Electric waves

While studying at the Livorno Technical Institute in 1894, Guglielmo read an article about communication occurring without the use of wires. He learned about the **pioneering** work of scientists James Clerk Maxwell and Heinrich Hertz. In 1873 Clerk Maxwell had **predicted** the existence of invisible electric waves in the air. In 1887 Heinrich Hertz found them. The waves became known as "Hertzian waves." Guglielmo was fascinated by this work.

Morse code

Morse code was named after Samuel Morse, the American who invented it in 1838. The code was used to send messages on land and at sea. When a message was received, it was decoded and turned back into letters. By the time of World War II, long after Samuel Morse had died, his code was still being used. Morse stations were essential for sending and receiving important wartime messages.

THE YOUNG SCIENTIST

Guglielmo Marconi wanted to carry out his own experiments with electricity, particularly with Hertzian waves. When he was about 19, he met Professor Augusto Righi, who was an expert in **wireless** waves. Righi taught **physics** at the University of Bologna in Italy, and he let Marconi use his **laboratory** there and study in the library.

The Villa Griffone laboratory

Marconi was not a student at the university, so it was impossible for him to do the kind of experiments he wanted. To do that, he needed a laboratory of his own. In 1894 the attic at the Villa Griffone became Marconi's home laboratory. He was encouraged by his mother, but his father disapproved. Eventually, Giuseppe Marconi did pay for his son's equipment—but only after making his son explain what he was trying to do.

Marconi's attic laboratory has been recreated at the Villa Griffone for visitors to see.

New ideas

Marconi wanted to make the mysterious Hertzian waves, so he repeated Hertz's experiments. Just like Hertz, he built a device to **transmit** the waves to a receiving device, called a spark-gap receiver. Marconi knew he had succeeded in making the silent, invisible waves, because when they arrived at the receiver they made a spark of electricity. The spark jumped across a short gap and made a crackling sound. It was a successful experiment, but Marconi had a better idea for the receiver. He replaced the spark-gap receiver with a device called a coherer.

The coherer

The coherer was a glass tube filled with **metal filings**. When Hertzian waves hit it, they made the metal filings stick, or cohere, together.

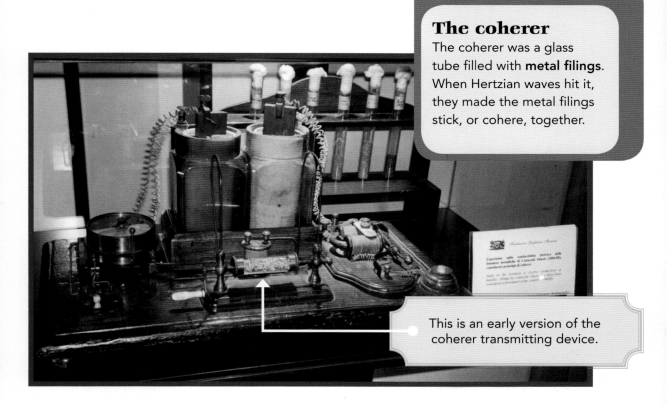

This is an early version of the coherer transmitting device.

Radio waves

"Hertzian waves" is the original name for **"radio waves."** Scientists, including Marconi, eventually dropped the term "Hertzian" and replaced it with "radio."

Marconi's brother Alfonso helped him with his experiments.

On/off signals

Marconi was interested in how the metal filings in a coherer tube behaved. When they were struck by Hertzian waves, they jumped around and stuck together. When the waves stopped, the filings fell down. They were behaving like a switch—"on" when the Hertzian waves were in the air, and "off" when there were none around.

A brilliant idea

Marconi knew that Morse code was actually a series of on/off signals. He wondered if he could use Hertzian waves to carry Morse code signals through the air, instead of along wires. It was a brilliant idea. As the Hertzian waves hit the coherer, the metal filings would behave in an on/off pattern that could be tapped out as Morse code and then converted back into letters. He told Professor Righi about his idea. Righi said it would never work. But the expert was wrong.

"Dot dot dot"

In the summer of 1895, Marconi used a Morse transmitter to tap out "dot dot dot" from his attic laboratory. This was Morse code for the letter "S." Alfonso, Marconi's brother, was 1 mile (1.6 kilometers) away from the Villa Griffone, waiting with a Morse code receiver attached to a coherer. The Hertzian waves carrying the "S" signal reached the coherer, and a tiny hammer jumped into action, tapping out the three dot sounds. Marconi had sent the world's first wireless, or radio, signal.

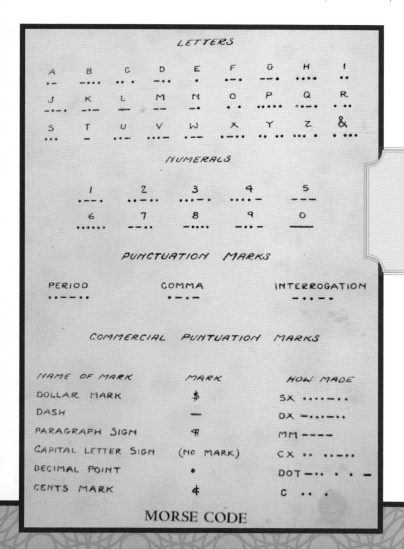

MORSE CODE

Marconi made use of Morse code as he developed wireless techonology. His first transmission was the three dots of the letter "S."

Marconi Moves to England

Guglielmo had proved that it was possible to send Morse code signals through the air. But he knew that it would not be long before other scientists—maybe in a university or a telegraphy company—also discovered the secret of **wireless** communication. He had to act fast, or someone else could take the credit for the discovery of this exciting new way to send messages.

Rejection

Guglielmo's parents came to his help. His father, Giuseppe, who had once hoped Guglielmo would get a job in the Italian navy, could now see the importance of his work. According to a family story, the Marconi family wrote to the Italian Ministry of Post and **Telegraph**. His family thought that if anyone would be interested in wireless, it would be this government department, as it was their job to deal with the country's postal and telegraph system. How wrong they were. After months of waiting, the Marconis were told that wireless had no future. Guglielmo felt he had been rejected by his own country.

Another chance?

All was not lost. Guglielmo's mother, Annie, still had friends and family in London. Annie thought that they might be able to persuade the English to take her son's discovery seriously. Guglielmo and his mother arrived in England in February 1896. With them were two black boxes containing Guglielmo's precious wireless equipment.

In the 1890s, city streets were criss-crossed by overhead telegraph wires.

Why England?

Marconi went to England not only because his mother knew people there, but also because it was the center of world shipping. He thought that shipping companies would be interested in wireless, as their ships could then send messages while they were at sea.

Marconi's magic boxes

Marconi's idea for wireless was taken seriously in England. His cousin, Henry Jameson-Davis, was an **engineer** who invited his friends to see Marconi's invention. Among them was Alan Campbell Swinton, an expert in electricity and its uses. Swinton was impressed and arranged for Marconi to meet William Preece, chief electrical engineer of the British Post Office.

Signals through walls!

On March 31, 1896, Marconi showed Preece his wireless system. Preece had never seen anything like it, and over the next few weeks he invited Marconi to show it to other post office officials. Marconi sent Morse code signals across the London sky to a receiver, where they were tapped out as letters by a printer. What amazed the officials most of all was that the signals went through solid walls!

William Preece helped Marconi start up wireless communication in England.

The British Post Office

The British Post Office was in charge of sending telegraphic messages. Preece could see that wireless communication was going to be important, and he hoped that Marconi would work with him to develop a wireless **network** for the post office.

Public demonstration

Preece had been working on his own method of wireless communication, but he saw that Marconi's was better. It was more powerful, sent signals over longer distances, and was cheaper. Preece decided to support Marconi.

On December 12, 1896, Preece and Marconi gave the first public demonstration of wireless. An audience in London's Toynbee Hall watched—and listened—as Preece pressed a lever inside one of Marconi's "magic boxes." It sent out a wireless signal, making a bell ring inside a box held by Marconi. London audiences were used to magic shows, but this was not a trick.

Marconi poses in 1896 with his early radio equipment.

The Bristol Channel tests

A major test for Marconi's invention came in May 1897, when William Preece asked him to send signals across the Bristol Channel, a body of water in southwest Britain. In all his tests to date, Marconi had only sent wireless signals over land. Now he would find out if wireless signals could be sent over water.

Success!

Marconi tried for two days. It was starting to look like failure, but on day three, May 13, 1897, Preece watched his Morse code receiver spring to life and print out the message: "ARE YOU READY." Marconi's message had traveled 3.5 miles (5.6 kilometers) across water. The tests continued, and on May 18, Marconi sent wireless messages across a wider part of the Bristol Channel— a distance of 8.7 miles (14 kilometers).

Sending wireless messages over water was incredibly important. It meant that ships could now keep in touch with the land when they were far out at sea, and with each other. Before wireless, ships used flashing lights or flags to send messages. These methods only worked when ships were in sight of land, and in clear weather.

News of Marconi's success spread, and other scientists began to build their own wireless equipment. Marconi knew this would happen, so he took out **patents**. He did not want others to make money from his invention.

Patents

Marconi used patents to protect his work from theft. They were **legal** documents issued to him, stopping others from stealing his ideas by copying them. Marconi had to prove his invention presented something new and did not copy existing work that had already been patented.

This drawing illustrates Marconi's 1897 Bristol Channel experiments.

Waves Across the Ocean

Marconi decided to concentrate on making **wireless** work at sea. He was confident that the world's shipping companies and navies would buy it, as it meant they could keep in touch with their ships. For this to work, Marconi needed wireless stations on land, where operators would send and receive signals to and from the ships.

The first wireless station

Marconi built the world's first wireless station in 1897, on the Isle of Wight, off the south coast of England. Other stations soon followed, and in 1899 he sent a signal across the English Channel, a large body of water between England and France, to a wireless station on the coast of northern France—a distance of 32 miles (52 kilometers).

Marconi's first wireless station was here at the Royal Needles Hotel on the Isle of Wight.

Poldhu to St. John's

Marconi wanted to send wireless messages between Europe and North America. In 1901 he built wireless stations at Poldhu, Cornwall, England, and St. John's, Newfoundland, Canada. Early in the afternoon of December 12, 1901, wireless waves crossed the Atlantic Ocean. Marconi, listening at the St. John's station, heard three clicks in his earpiece—Morse code for the letter "S." The signal had traveled 1,800 miles (2,880 kilometers).

In his own words

"I now felt for the first time absolutely certain that the day would come when mankind would be able to send messages without wires not only across the Atlantic but between the farthermost ends of the Earth."

Guglielmo Marconi

Before the test, he had been criticized by scientists who said it would never work. They said wireless signals could only travel in straight lines, but over very long distances the signals would have to bend around the curve of Earth—and that is exactly what they did. The critics were silenced.

Marconi (in the far left of the photo) is watching **engineers** set up the wireless equipment at St. John's, Newfoundland, in December 1901.

Fame and fortune

Marconi was just 27 years old when he sent the first trans-Atlantic wireless signal. As news spread around the world, he became rich and famous.

Italian roots

Although Marconi was living and working in England, he had not forgotten his Italian roots—and Italy had not forgotten him. In 1902 he was asked to join the king of Italy on board his warship, the *Carlo Alberto*, as it sailed from England to Italy. Marconi set up a wireless station on the ship, and that September he received a message from the Poldhu transmitter in England. To reach Italy, the wireless signal had cut through bad weather and through mountains.

Leaders from other nations were just as quick to recognize the importance of wireless. For example, in January 1903, Theodore Roosevelt, the president of the United States, sent a wireless message to King Edward VII of Great Britain. In the message, President Roosevelt described wireless as a "wonderful triumph."

ing that this policy worked upon the feelings of the people with the result that enormous sums were voted for naval defence.

WIRELESS TELEGRAPHY ACROSS THE ATLANTIC.

(FROM OUR CORRESPONDENT.)

ST. JOHNS, N.F., DEC. 14.

Signor Marconi authorizes me to announce that he received on Wednesday and Thursday electrical signals at his experimental station here from the station at Poldhu, Cornwall, thus solving the problem of telegraphing across the Atlantic without wires. He has informed the

This is the newspaper announcement of the first trans-Atlantic wireless signal.

Family life

In 1905 Marconi married Beatrice O'Brien. She was the daughter of a wealthy Irishman, Edward Donough O'Brien, whose family had been kings of Ireland until the 1500s. Guglielmo and Beatrice had three daughters (one of whom lived only a few weeks) and a son.

Marconigram

When an operator received a wireless message, he changed the Morse code into letters and words. He wrote them out on a form, and a postman delivered it to the person the message was for. These messages sent between wireless stations became known as Marconigrams.

This photograph of Beatrice, Marconi's first wife, was taken in 1907.

Wireless to the Rescue

On a foggy morning in January 1909, two ships collided off the east coast of the United States. The British ship *Republic*, carrying about 1,600 passengers, was rammed by an Italian vessel, the *Florida*, and started to sink. She was a luxury liner, and her owners had fitted her out with the very latest communication equipment—a Marconi **wireless** station.

The *Republic*'s wireless operator tapped out in Morse code the distress signal, CQD (CQ for "All Stations, Attention," and D for "Distress"). It was the first wireless distress signal ever sent by a sinking ship, and it was a life-saver. Seven ships heard the signal and came to the rescue of the *Republic*'s passengers. The Marconi wireless station had saved lives.

The *Republic* was a floating palace before she was struck by the *Florida*.

Winning the Nobel Prize

In the same year, Marconi was given the highest possible honor. He was awarded the **Nobel Prize** for **Physics**, which he shared with Karl Braun. Braun was one of Marconi's rivals who had also been developing wireless communication. The judges decided that both scientists had done equally important work, and the prize was shared between them.

Catching criminals

Wireless caused a sensation in 1910 when it was used to catch Dr. Hawley Crippen. He was wanted in England for murder. Crippen tried to escape to Canada, but the captain of the ship he was sailing on recognized him. Captain Henry Kendall sent a famous wireless message to the British police, and when his ship reached Canada, Crippen was arrested, sent back to England, and hanged.

Captain Kendall's wireless message

"Have strong suspicions that Crippen London cellar murderer and accomplice are among saloon passengers."

Henry Kendall,
Captain of the *Montrose*

Dr. Crippen was wanted for murdering his wife.

The *Titanic* disaster

Three years after the sinking of the *Republic*, another ocean liner sank in the Atlantic—the *Titanic*. In April 1912 the *Titanic* sailed from Southampton, England, on her maiden (first) voyage to New York. There were approximately 2,200 men, women, and children on board. On April 14, after four days at sea, her Marconi wireless operators received messages from nearby ships warning her of icebergs. The *Titanic* sailed on. Then, as midnight approached, a lookout shouted: "Iceberg, right ahead!"

The liner's starboard (right) side scraped against the ice mountain, splitting her hull open below the waterline. The ship's wireless operators frantically tapped out the Morse code CQD distress signal, then switched over to SOS—the first time this signal had been used by a ship.

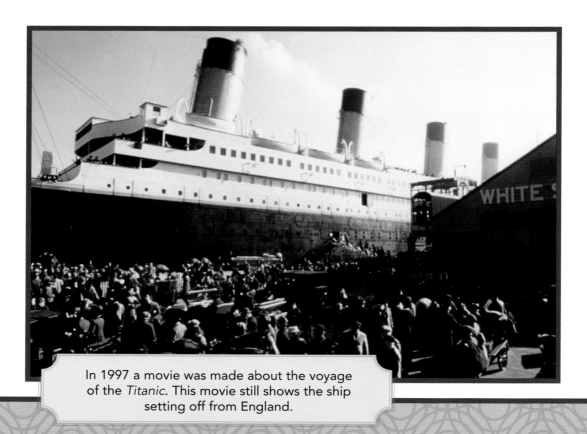

In 1997 a movie was made about the voyage of the *Titanic*. This movie still shows the ship setting off from England.

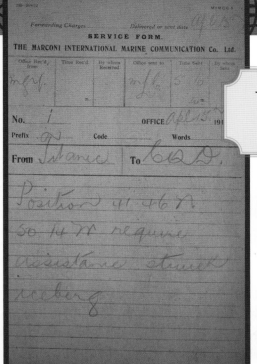

This is the actual message (left) that was sent from the radio room on board the *Titanic* (right) using Morse code.

The *Carpathia*

As dawn broke on the morning of April 15, the liner *Carpathia* arrived at the scene. The *Titanic* had sunk without a trace, and there were only 706 survivors for the *Carpathia* to rescue. Marconi's wireless had saved them, and it flashed news of the disaster around the world.

Marconi and his family had been due to sail on the *Titanic* but, luckily for them, they had canceled their plans. Instead, Marconi went to New York on a different ship. When the *Carpathia* arrived with the *Titanic* survivors, Marconi was there to see them come ashore.

CQD and SOS

The first Morse code distress signal was CQD, introduced in 1904. In 1908 an international agreement brought a new signal into use—SOS. Eventually SOS replaced the CQD signal. SOS is often said to stand for "Save our Souls," but in fact it was simply a convenient way to remember the Morse code needed.

MARCONI AT WAR

In 1914 World War I began. It lasted four terrible years and involved countries from around the world. On one side were Great Britain, France, and their **allies**, and on the other were Germany, Austria, and their allies. Italy did not get involved until 1915, when it joined Britain and France. The United States joined the same side in 1917.

The assassination of Archduke Ferdinand of Austria in 1914 led to World War I.

Marconi was an Italian citizen, and even though Italy was on Britain's side, he was viewed with suspicion because he was a foreigner. He volunteered to fight for Italy, and the British government allowed him to leave Britain—but only after it had taken over his **wireless** factory and wireless stations. The government knew that wireless was going to be very important in the war, and it wanted to control its use.

Casualties of World War I

- 8 million killed
- 21 million wounded
- 2 million missing

Marconi in the army

Marconi joined the Italian army and was put in charge of its wireless **network**. He improved the mobile wireless stations that soldiers used on the battlefield. Marconi also helped the Italian navy and air force. For the navy, he invented a method of sending secret wireless messages between warships. For the air force, he invented a wireless telephone system that allowed pilots to communicate with people on the ground.

The war ended in 1918. The Italian government recognized that Marconi had served his country well, and that wireless had played a very important part in the war effort. In 1919 he was awarded the Military Medal—a high honor. That same year he represented Italy as a **diplomat** at a conference in Paris, France, when the world's leaders came together to sign a peace treaty.

This photograph shows Marconi in his Italian army uniform during World War I.

Singing through space

Marconi had spent most of his time and effort on developing the Morse code use of wireless, but as early as 1900 another use had been found for it. In that year, Reginald Fessenden, a Canadian scientist, had used wireless waves to **transmit** the human voice, and in 1906 he had made the first broadcast of speech and music. This marked the beginning of radio.

As the world recovered after World War I, it became clear to Marconi that people wanted to hear the human voice over the airwaves. The "dit-dit-dit" and "dah-dah-dah" clicks of Morse code would still have their use, especially for ships, but for ordinary people, radio was the future.

On June 15, 1920, Marconi made the world's first radio broadcast of live entertainment for the public. It came from his radio studio at Chelmsford, England, and starred Dame Nellie Melba, a famous Australian opera singer. She sang three well-known songs. Wireless operators throughout Europe were advised to listen in between 7 and 8 p.m., when they would hear Dame Nellie "'singing through space." Her voice was heard 1,000 miles (1,600 kilometers) across Europe, and by ships at sea.

The era of radio broadcasting for the home had begun, and Marconi was determined to lead the way. He began making and selling receivers to the public. These were the first home radios.

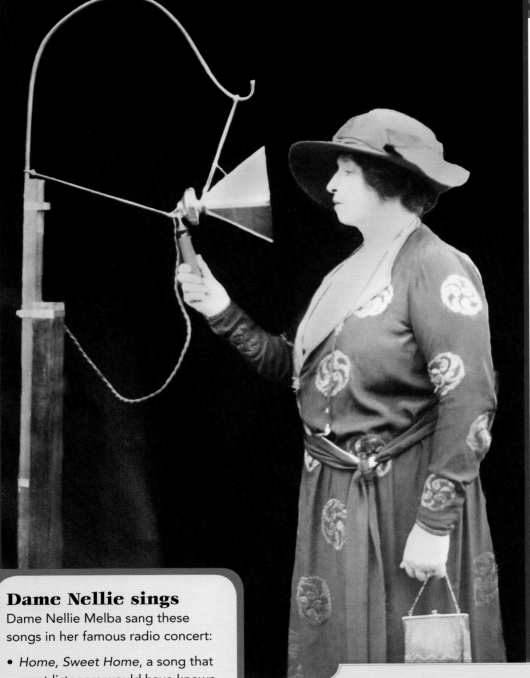

Dame Nellie sings

Dame Nellie Melba sang these songs in her famous radio concert:

- *Home, Sweet Home*, a song that most listeners would have known

- *Nymphs and Fauns*, a song to dance to

- *Addio*, a song from the opera *La Bohème*

Dame Nellie Melba broadcasts from the Marconi works at Chelmsford in 1920.

Marconi's yacht was a workplace for him as well as a place to entertain guests.

Life at sea

At about the same time as he was **pioneering** radio broadcasts, Marconi was building a **laboratory** with a difference. In 1919 he bought a yacht, the *Rovenska*, for 21,000 British pounds (about $1.3 million in today's money). It was a big, white yacht, 220 feet (67 meters) long, powered by steam engines. It had once belonged to the royal family of Austria, but they had sold it to a British businessman. During World War I, the British navy had used the *Rovenska* to search for **enemy mines** in the English Channel.

The floating laboratory

Marconi renamed the yacht *Elettra*. He turned it into a floating laboratory, from which he carried out wireless experiments. The *Elettra*, which had a crew of 30, became Marconi's home at sea, complete with its own grand piano! Guests came to stay, including the kings of England, Spain, and Italy. Marconi's children loved the *Elettra*, but his wife, Beatrice, did not. Guglielmo and Beatrice were not happily married, and their marriage ended in 1924.

In the mid-1920s, Marconi became a friend and supporter of Benito Mussolini, the prime minister of Italy. Mussolini treated him as an Italian hero, and Marconi liked the attention this brought him.

Marconi and Mussolini

Mussolini ruled Italy as a **dictator**. He was feared by many, and Marconi lost friends because of his support for Mussolini. For example, in 1935, when Mussolini sent the Italian army into Ethiopia, the British government refused to let Marconi make a radio broadcast supporting the invasion.

Marconi (right) stands with the Italian prime minister, Benito Mussolini (left).

Marconi's Final Years

Marconi's life changed considerably in 1927. That summer, he married for the second time. His new wife was Maria Cristina Bezzi-Scali, the daughter of an Italian **nobleman**.

The Imperial Wireless Chain

Toward the end of the year, Marconi completed the Imperial **Wireless** Chain for the British government. It was used to send long-distance messages between Britain, Canada, Australia, South Africa, and India. Marconi soon added Argentina, Brazil, the United States, and Japan to the chain of countries connected by wireless.

Marconi and his second wife, Maria Cristina Bezzi-Scali, are shown here on his yacht *Elettra*. This photograph was taken the year that Marconi died.

Thousands of people attended Marconi's funeral, which was held in Bologna.

This international **network** used powerful wireless stations called beam stations. Morse code messages were "beamed" between them, traveling at the speed of light. Light travels at about 186,000 miles (300,000 kilometers) per second. Messages were received almost as soon as they had been sent.

Marconi had worked hard all his life, and the strain eventually affected his health. Late in 1927 he suffered a heart attack. He recovered, but his heart was weakened. He began to spend more time with Maria Cristina and less time on his experiments. In 1930 the couple had a daughter.

Lighting up Sydney

In March 1930, Marconi managed to send electricity by **radiotelegraphy** from Genoa, Italy, all the way to Sydney, Australia. The electricity was used to switch on about 2,000 electric light bulbs inside Sydney City Hall.

In 1933 the family set off on an around-the-world cruise on board the yacht *Elettra*. After their cruise, they returned to Italy and set up home in Rome, the country's capital. It was here, on July 20, 1937, that Marconi died, at age 63. In the days that followed, countries around the world held radio silences out of respect for Guglielmo Marconi.

Was Marconi really the "father of radio"?

Guglielmo Marconi is often described as the "father of radio"—but is this true? It might be better to call him "one of the fathers of radio." Many scientists played a part in the creation of the wireless, or radio, as it came to be known. Marconi studied the work of others and used it in his own work. It was like doing a very complicated jigsaw puzzle, with many people searching for the pieces to complete the picture. Marconi was just one of those people.

There is no doubt that Marconi was a talented scientist, but he was also a talented businessman. He believed that he could make wireless a worldwide success, and that is exactly what happened.

Wireless who's who

- 1873: James Clerk Maxwell **predicted** the existence of electric waves.

- 1887: Heinrich Hertz discovered Clerk Maxwell's electric waves (Hertzian waves).

- 1893: Nikola Tesla claimed to have invented a method of sending messages without wires.

- 1894: Oliver Lodge communicated using Hertzian waves.

- May 1895: Alexander Popov used Hertzian waves to **transmit** a signal.

- August 1895: Guglielmo Marconi used Hertzian waves to transmit a signal.

- 1900: Reginald Fessenden sent the first voice message by wireless.

- 1906: Lee De Forest improved the broadcast of live radio.

His companies spread wireless technology—and his name—around the world. Wireless messages became known as Marconigrams, but the names of other scientists quietly faded away. (Heinrich Hertz's "Hertzian waves," which made wireless possible, became "**radio waves**.")

Guglielmo Marconi was an innovator—a person whose work, added to that of others, helped him connect the many pieces of the wireless puzzle.

Nikola Tesla: The forgotten inventor

Nikola Tesla (1856–1943) was born in Croatia and emigrated to the United States in 1884. He was an electrical **engineer** and, like Marconi, was a pioneer of wireless communications. Tesla said he had sent messages without wires as early as 1893, two years before Marconi sent his famous first signal. To protect his many wireless inventions, Tesla took out **patents**. When Marconi sent his wireless signal across the Atlantic Ocean in 1901, he did it using some of Tesla's inventions. Marconi said he had come up with the same ideas himself, but Tesla felt Marconi had copied him. In 1943 the U.S. Supreme Court agreed with Tesla, and because of this many people believe he is the real "father of radio," not Marconi.

Marconi's legacy

The world has become a noisier place, thanks to Marconi. In 1896, when he demonstrated his "magic boxes" to an audience in London's Toynbee Hall, he wanted them to hear the sound of a bell being rung by the invisible power of wireless. It was the world's first ringtone. Today's theater and movie audiences are politely requested to switch off their cell phones. Marconi would be amazed to know that his bell was the **ancestor** of today's noisy ringtones!

The airwaves are alive with the invisible, silent power of wireless technology. When we turn a radio dial, we hear speech and music coming to us from around the globe. Televisions and computers can tune in to radio stations and, of course, they bring us pictures, too. Bored with the channel? Then point and press the remote control, making the picture change. There are no wires between you and the TV—that is wireless technology in action.

International Marconi Day

International Marconi Day is held each year on the Saturday closest to Marconi's birthday (April 25). On this day amateur radio operators contact each other from places where Marconi wireless stations used to exist. The radio operators use wireless techniques similar to those used by Marconi.

Wireless technology today

What else has Marconi done for us? Perhaps the greatest advancement in wireless technology today is in the world of computers. The Internet joins the world's millions of PCs, laptops, game consoles, music players, and phones together in a worldwide network. More and more access to the Internet is made by wireless technology.

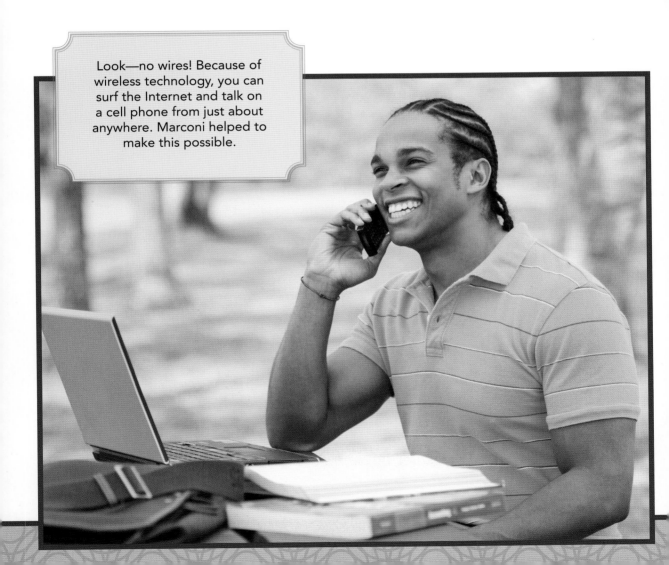

Look—no wires! Because of wireless technology, you can surf the Internet and talk on a cell phone from just about anywhere. Marconi helped to make this possible.

TIMELINES

Marconi's life

APRIL 25, 1874   Guglielmo Marconi is born in Bologna, northern Italy

1895   Marconi **transmits wireless** signals at Villa Griffone, his home in Italy

1896   Marconi moves to London. He **patents** his wireless system and demonstrates wireless at Toynbee Hall.

1897   Marconi sets up the Wireless **Telegraph** and Signal Company. He transmits a wireless signal across the Bristol Channel.

1898   Marconi opens the world's first factory to make wireless equipment, at Chelmsford, England

1899   Marconi transmits a wireless signal across the English Channel, from England to France

1901   Marconi transmits a wireless signal across the Atlantic Ocean, from England to Canada

1905   Marconi marries Beatrice O'Brien

1908   Marconi's daughter Degna is born

1909   Marconi shares the **Nobel Prize** for **Physics**

1910   Marconi's son Giulio is born

1914   Marconi wireless stations in Britain are taken over by the British government in World War I

1915   Marconi joins the Italian army, in World War I

1916   Marconi moves to the Italian navy, in World War I. His daughter Gioia is born.

1919   Marconi attends the Paris Peace Conference as a **diplomat** for Italy. He is awarded the Italian Military Medal. He buys a yacht and turns it into a floating **laboratory**.

1920   Dame Nellie Melba makes the world's first public broadcast program, from the Marconi works at Chelmsford

1922   The British Broadcasting Company (BBC) is formed by Marconi and five other companies

1924   Marconi's marriage to Beatrice ends

1927   Marconi marries Maria Cristina Bezzi-Scali. Countries around the world become part of the Imperial Wireless Chain.

1930   Marconi's daughter Elettra is born

JULY 20, 1937   Marconi dies in Rome, Italy

World timeline

1814	Joseph Nicéphore Niépce takes the first photograph
1831	Joseph Henry invents the electric telegraph
1838	Samuel Morse invents Morse code
1843	Alexander Bain invents the fax machine
1866	The first successful Atlantic telegraph cable is laid, connecting the United Kingdom and the United States
1876	Alexander Graham Bell invents the electric telephone
1877	Thomas Edison invents the **phonograph**. Eadweard Muybridge takes the first moving pictures.
1887	Emile Berliner invents the **gramophone**
1901	Guglielmo Marconi transmits the first radio signal across the Atlantic Ocean
1914	The first telephone call between continents is made
1925	John Logie Baird transmits the first television signal
1927	The first television broadcasts are made in the United Kingdom
1930	The first television broadcasts are made in the United States
1944	The first computers come into use
1958	Chester Carlson invents the photocopier
1969	ARPAnet—the first Internet—begins. It is a **network** of military computers in the United States.
1971	The computer floppy disc is invented. The computer microprocessor is invented, and the first email is sent.
1979	The first mobile phone network begins, in Japan
1984	The Apple Macintosh computer is released. The IBM PC is released.
1994	The Internet becomes available worldwide to private users

GLOSSARY

allies people, countries, or organizations that have agreed to help each other

ancestor family member who lived in the past

conductor material that allows heat, light, sound, or electricity to pass along it or through it

dictator ruler who has an unlimited amount of power—usually a person who has taken control by force

diplomat person who represents his or her country abroad, who usually works for the government

electrophysics area of physics that studies electricity

enemy mine bomb that floats in water, designed to explode when a ship sails into it

engineer person who is skilled at working with machines or engines

gramophone machine that plays back sound recordings made on records (flat discs with grooves)

laboratory room used for scientific experiments

legal anything to do with the law

metal filings tiny pieces of metal

network group, set, or chain of devices that are all linked together

Nobel Prize annual award for outstanding achievement in six subject areas. The subject areas are: physics, chemistry, medicine, literature, economics, and peace.

nobleman person who belongs to the upper class of society

patent official document that registers a person's idea for an invention. It is a way of recognizing that the idea for the invention belongs to that person, and to no one else.

phonograph machine that plays back sound recordings made on cylinders

physics scientific study of matter and energy—for example, heat, light, and sound

pioneering doing something that no one has done before

predict tell the future

radio waves form of invisible energy that is used to carry messages through the air

radiotelegraphy use of radio to send telegraphic messages

telegraph message sent in code along wires and cables

telegraphist person who was trained to send and receive messages sent by telegraph. The messages were in Morse code.

transmit send something

wireless without the need for wires or cables

Want to Know More?

Books

Goldsmith, Mike. *Guglielmo Marconi (Scientists Who Made History)*. Chicago: Raintree, 2002.

Sonneborn, Liz. *Guglielmo Marconi: Inventor of Wireless Technology*. New York: Franklin Watts, 2005.

Zannos, Susan. *Guglielmo Marconi and Radio Waves*. Hockessin, Del.: Mitchell Lane, 2004.

Websites

www.fgm.it
The Guglielmo Marconi Foundation is located in the Marconi family home, Villa Griffone, in Italy. You can click at the bottom of the home page for text in English.

www.marconicalling.com
Marconi's story is presented by the Marconi Corporation. The website includes a film clip showing Marconi on his way to meet the survivors of the *Titanic* disaster in 1912, and lots of photographs of early radios.

www.pbs.org/wgbh/aso/databank/entries/btmarc.html
This PBS site features a biography of Marconi as well as interactive features that explore "Technology at Home" and "Radio Transmission."

Places of interest

The U.S. Marconi Museum, Bedford, New Hampshire
A museum dedicated to Marconi with exhibits featuring equipment, literature, and audio-visual presentations, as well as an extensive technical library.

Villa Griffone, near Bologna, Italy
The birthplace of wireless, with a Marconi museum on site.

Marconi Center, Poldhu, Cornwall, England
The location of Marconi's historic 1901 trans-Atlantic wireless signal, with a Marconi museum on site.

INDEX